Journey Through the Fire

by

Julie Stevens

First published 2024 by The Hedgehog Poetry Press,

5 Coppack House, Churchill Avenue, Clevedon. BS21 6QW

www.hedgehogpress.co.uk

Copyright © Julie Stevens 2024

The right of Julie Stevens to be identified as the author of this work has been asserted in accordance with the Copyright, Designs and Patents Act 1988. All rights reserved. No part of this publication may be reproduced, stored in or introduced into a retrieval system, or transmitted in any form, or by any means (electronic, mechanical, photocopying, recording or otherwise) without prior written permissions of the publisher. Any person who does any unauthorised act in relation to this publication may be liable for criminal prosecution and civil claims for damages.

ISBN: 978-1-916830-21-9

Contents

Dementia	5
Them	6
Pink	7
Wolf Class	8
Badger Watch	9
Bully	10
Earthquake	11
Guilt	12
Piano Practice	13
Why I Don't Like Kippers	14
Steam	15
Control	16
Tidal Wave	17
My Next Move	18
Letting Go	19
Refuel	20
Nerves	21
Boulder	22
Sun Snake	23
Swallow	24
Swamp	25
To the Fire	26
Full Of Green	27
Autograph Book	28
Is it Grief?	29
Smoulder	30
Unravelling	31
Is this the Future?	32
Hold Fire	33
Finding Our Cure	34
Acknowledgements	36

DEMENTIA

I carried memories of our lives
and taught them how to be,
how to take each speck of time
nurture it, hold it ready.

I carried memories of our lives
and placed them in egg cups,
in front of her hands.
I asked her to wait and watch.

I tapped and tapped
encouraged the crack,
knew how a memory would die
if it didn't find the light.

I saw a memory appear,
a finger emerged from the shell
and I gave it to her.
Now she knew.

THEM

I lived with the volume high,
anchored between their protests
and stillness,
which never turned them off.
I lived with my head buried –
I didn't want to take
their problems with me,
nor judge and deliver
the awful verdict.
The shouting floored the house.
The sudden lurch of a room
knocked me into a bedroom cell.
I lived with their weapons,
their fights;
conflicts were nailed down hard
in my head.
The fear of what could come next
was always present.
It lived with me,
but the real me
was never there.

PINK

I sat on the pile of cushions
that let me escape
to the story
and launched the pink one
straight at my teacher.

That was *her colour* back at home –
her maternal dress code full of pink.
Miss was shocked. I was shocked.
My stifled mind lashed out
at the wrong person
with a pink dressed arm
shaped *by you.*
Always shaped *by you.*
Were my ideas not good enough?

I wonder if my teacher could tell
I was trying to climb out,
or did she just see
a naughty school girl
who threw a cushion?

7

WOLF CLASS

I felt the roar as thirty children swamped the field
their eyes towards the guard of trees,
their legs kicking back my wish to follow.

One rallied sprint as spiteful wolves
to an untamed place that held no rules
except one: leave me standing alone.

Nine years old with the weight of them all
with the hurt of knowing I couldn't join in,
with the stench of a classroom riddled with taunts.

The flicker of shadows between trunks and branches
one dark wave from a deserter's hand,
one single body who wanted to confess.

A friend who tore their game apart,
a friend who spat out their dark secret.
One fearless friend who couldn't digest the carnage.

BADGER WATCH

The eyes stop you. I hadn't thrown on
enough layers to keep them back.
Their arctic glare churned my blood to ice,
each shard, a dagger sharpened.
I had thought badgers were a soft option.
Their black, white build, a fluffy, fuzzy soothe,
like the rub of kittens, who could always
make a room blush.
The air timed this chill,
threw a raw sheet over the exact moment
the ground felt more uncomfortable.
I'd waited far too long on this hard lump of mud.
Watch a badger,
see it surface was my aim,
but I wasn't convinced those eyes
were badger eyes.
I began to wonder. Who was staring back?

BULLY

Ember, they called her.
Hair flowing blond, so long
it always left a mark.
Never without a gang of boys
sidling up to hold her hand.

Stood in a classroom
hearing raw gossip from friends
whose tongues caught fire.
One lunchtime, a time to talk
and revisit rumours

racing to the front,
that could never be silenced
in our minds,
or left to simmer
on a hand that punched.

It sprang like a knife
cutting pieces of why,
screeching pain that couldn't reason,
stunned mouths
my tunnel to slump in.

She left. Sauntered away,
like a film star who'd kissed
their opening lines. No remorse.
Just a line of muddy footprints
bruising the floor.

EARTHQUAKE

Her eyes were marbles caught in your throat
and her smile was a coffin nailed tight
and her hair was spaghetti hanging
and her ears were horns packed with hardened cement.
Her tongue was a knife dropped on a foot
and her laugh was a crow trapped in a bin
and her teeth were razor blades lining a boot
and her eyelashes were telegraph poles obscuring the valley.
Her finger was a tennis bat whacking sixty lit matches
and her opinions were enough to sink a cruise liner
and her words were snooker cues without chalk
and her blouses were wallpaper peeling.
The last time they spoke
it was an earthquake with one survivor.

GUILT

I didn't cower in the corner and dismiss their words,
there was always something inside
that wouldn't stop throbbing.
The voice of the dare would constantly prod
until I'd scream from the rooftop,
I'm listening!
I saw the twist of flames, the fire, then the rug,
paper in hand, I wanted to try.
One scorched hole later, the stench of fear.
That stare from pink ted, the devil in those eyes,
it hurt when they didn't find me.
I yanked them out. Can you see me now?
The egg on your door, a trick or a treat?
A morning glow, the sun would scream.
They warned me about playing with boys.
I caved in. There's still a loud cry
from childhood years that found a voice.
I can still hear them holler.

PIANO PRACTICE

It's never black and white.
Each note may wrap you in the skin of a newborn,
scratch at years with a harrowing call
or send you humming through the doors at work.
When she played, the piano sent time scurrying
to find hours that the day had lost,
pages that were never read and light
now dimming, losing centre stage.
A master of the keys was her doing
waking a night with the clutch of Brahms,
Debussy winding through each morning's stretch
and another three hours packed with fingers alight.
For years it was always her
bringing the whip to my young hands,
a bleeding insight into notes that waited,
a battle to race with those elegant turns.
They'd stand behind singing words to celebrate
call on me to find music to cheer,
but all I felt was the sting of their breath
shooting syllables into broken fingers.

WHY I DON'T LIKE KIPPERS

I sensed they were coming
when the stench rose up the staircase –
a flood of foul-smelling slime
that knew just how to net me.

Noxious flapping, dives and smoky fins
around they went, swamped today's sweet breath.
She urged me to try this ocean sick,
swore a healthy body should be full of gills,
that I should swim by her side, copy her ways,
hook a life with only her in charge.

A wave of hate saw me jump through portholes,
my belly would retch, whilst on this sea bed.
A call from downstairs made me slide on scales,
washed me nearer my salty seat.
I sat, I moaned, found the perfect bowl of cereal,
but my spoon was always full of stinking kippers.

STEAM

That house was a cauldron
in which they boiled
who I was.
My name was thrown in,
my beloved clothes
and music that hugged me.
Soaked, suffocated
as they tried to speak out.
Every ingredient sank
to be stirred
with a stay silent potion.
Anyone who tried
to free my entombed mind
rose in steam
and filled the room
with a stewed prison.
Treasured possessions,
words that protested,
books to flee
and rampant ideas,
all bubbling.
My freedom could only
be achieved
as a seething rage
rising through windows,
instead of being dumped
on the charred,
condemned base.

CONTROL

Imagine a box, body-sized and you're inside.
You can stand. Cramped. Just.
That's where I lived
and had to lug the thing around with me
everywhere I went.

Imagine having a voice
torn out as the words exit.
Ideas choke,
when there's too much build up.

Forget the clothes you long to wear,
they're still in the shop; the pile grows.
Thief hands are carving a shape for you,
material laid out; colours chosen. You'll hang
them up as dead weights. Wear them, cold.

Walk on the side of the road they tell you to,
only climb heights moulded by them.
End points will be planned in advance;
no discussion.
Don't try to leave the course. They'll find you.

The box still stands, but saggy and torn,
kept in the shed, a constant reminder,
a message to myself.

I stepped in yesterday. I almost burnt.
I left it today. A box on fire.

TIDAL WAVE

I didn't cry when they left.
It was the last time I'd see them
before the term capsized at Christmas.
My first day was all about cleaning.
The filth in my room had to be
scooped up, cast overboard she said,
scrubbed to make this cabin look younger.
Either that, or find a new boat and drop
my anchor again.
I thought it looked alright as it was
but she wouldn't let me set sail,
didn't even speak a word about this
buoyant ride – travelling forwards with
friends to create the right waves.
She wanted to clean.
She wanted to tear apart all that I had
before I even started to navigate.
He knew we shouldn't unload cargo
whilst cutting giant holes in safety nets.
He wanted to disembark, drown final hugs
and words that might, just might, encourage.
They motored away and left me
battling to hold my heavy oars.
I didn't cry, even though I needed to,
because this tidal wave had already
filled my mouth.

MY NEXT MOVE

For the first time I was alone.
My college room had me clothed
to protect from trials back home.
A separation would find my words.

This was my room. This was my bed
and there I sat, holding a phone card,
unnerving my fingers,
still ablaze with their lives.

I found life on a different seat
and placed my learning underneath,
where it couldn't be kicked away
to old days, where I was almost invisible.

Here, words could be spoken on screens
with letters to chant my next move,
or from a mobile phone
that never let you feel trapped.

Each year brought a fresh idea
how to interact in an unimaginable way,
whilst building a fort
to preserve this new mind.

LETTING GO

I can calm dark shadows, but only here,
where the trees unzip, let their leaves spin down
to warm the earth in a spread of gold.

A ballad so quiet, it will reel me in,
slide a memory to stalk this whispered mind
and open a time where these eyes can weep.

Here are the years that cut determined skin,
made young dreams bleed and take their warnings.
Here, where no one knew how to taste the sky.

I slip between trees standing naked in their graves,
each leaf a reminder, this trodden path will rise.
Every buried step now, must start a lonely climb.

REFUEL

It always comes back.
The swell of soil
as the sky blinds.

I walk by young stems
keeping the sun on my back
and follow this recovery.

The air feels less dense,
bright enough to end nightmares
that tumbled and slashed inside.

Snowdrops avoid the glare
know they will conjure renewed eyes –
spring's gathering of wintered bones.

An assured promise carried me here
to savour their arrival and plant some
healing in my bag.

Tired bodies always seize the call of spring.

NERVES

I didn't want to meet death, not just yet
but I thought it stood there, next to me.
Hospital scaffolding was alive with the wind —
metals poles rocked, like hostages, tied.
I clutched my head, as I edged to the right
away from one pole, I thought might swing,
drop, lay me out cold. This visit could count
weeks and not hours, and that's if my clock
didn't stop. With no time to think, I quick-stepped
under metal and ambled down the corridor stream —
aimed bulbs gleamed, like a surgeon's knife,
and lit my fear. I found a place in which to dwell
on electric currents, racing down an arm —
fingers gnarled — twisting with shock.
A scalpel to cut it out: masks, blood, hellish cries.
I think I'm imagining too much.
Tell me, what does a broken nerve look like?
As the door opened, I could almost hear
the swish of an axe.

BOULDER

It started as grit.
Sharp words from a doctor,
who couldn't smooth the outcome.
My body heavy, caked in sand
left, kicking back the dunes.
Each day a shake, each week a shovel
every year scratching skin
with lines I remembered.
Every year with a brush
trying to clean up his mess.
It journeyed with me, hurled together
as a sandstorm, firing me down.
Grit became pebble, became
a squatting rock, became a boulder
that confined me.
We heave, We shove
try to smash it in half,
but this illness slams shut,
holds you,
under a thumping hammer.

SUN SNAKE

Sun tips me off balance
unsettles the ride from spring,
throws a shadow over this carefree season.

The stifling heat controls the game,
will always block my way forward,
will make sure I can't compete.
Slap on some lotion, wear a hat
put up a defence to ward it off,
though it always snakes its way in
down these legs, round every muscle,
heat smoulders my attempts to move –
paralyses a tropical day.

Grab an ice cream, make a cold drink
find a shady space to hide,
but the sun will know where to find me.

SWALLOW

And I'm here being swallowed.
The sofa's mouth sucks me in,
dense air around pushes
its lead hand.

Forgive me, whilst I do nothing,
swallow every word,
forget the list, I never wrote.
Stare, like a traffic light,
through fogged voices.

Fatigue has shut my door
cancelled that slice of hope,
left my red beam cursing green.
I swallow that pile of jobs.

SWAMP

Nights are full of mud
packed with disease
that won't shift, or
ease the pain of moving
under a swamp duvet.
I heave through dirt
letting my eyes sink
with a mossy load.
Legs pick heavy fights
and a spine that's
soaked, twists a gift
to the night trolls –
broken nerves,
sliced by dark matter.
Dreams lie on wetland
bulging with decay
and are slit open
before they end.
You can watch them drown.

TO THE FIRE

On the doorstep, a face poisoned
full of years of advice.
Behind, I see walls and
remember what they meant.
They're stood on the same axis,
but swollen with worries.
Walls that guard stairs
I used to escape up,
try blot the explosions
huddled near a bed,
or sit sheltered
at the bottom
praying
they wouldn't storm down.
Part of me wanted to hear
what they screamed. Understand.
A sink nearby
where I could hide my tears.
Close that bloody door!
How the knives pierce.
As I step inside, I know
I'll wake the dark.

FULL OF GREEN

In a grubby green cardigan, he shelters with coffee
offers time to music, which is not to his taste.
The garden inside is a better sound.

A girl in apple-green stilettos staggers past.
Paints a running whiff of coffee
down his shoes. Her apple turns sour.
She barks at him. *Mind out the bloody way!*
Wipes her own loss and slumps, as far away
as the café allows.

Paintings line the wall, take my eyes
to green topiary, green conifers, green buds —
an escape to keep you alive.
Your cardigan will keep the leaves growing,
play your future, but steal my thoughts.
A mind empty, but full of green.

Stay in the warm old man. Green is safe here.
Your dangling threads can curl from cuffs
and soak up coffee. Catch the hour. Catch the years.
Hold that conifer and let it lift you,
walk those fields and charm the air.
I'm here, you're there and we are gathering green.

AUTOGRAPH BOOK

Lost voices cheer from a book
foaming with words.

Shrieks from a playground, a skip and banter
land on a page, that joked in silence
until now, when the paper's turned, blurry but alive
with backstage hustling, rhymes to amaze.

A holiday invites, pens dripping from the beach,
the smudge of suncream smearing their names.

Family lines charge through a musty blast,
names woken from those hidden years.

Sombre departures inked with care;
I can still smell Grandad's jacket.

IS IT GRIEF?

And is it grief when your legs buckle
has you lying in nettles
face in the dirt?

And is it grief that lays next to you
riddled with questions
as you try to sleep?

Does grief make you see people
on every surface —
a familiar face?

Has grief made you check,
charge to the door
to find it's locked?

Does grief make your hair shout
your clothes not match,
have you stalk every mirror?

When the box closes
lets the sunlight fly,
is this grief?

Does grief scratch your skin
let the rivers run
to show the colour?

Because why am I here
searching for answers
I've already found?

SMOTHER

When you threw flames
I caught them,
let them burn my hands
until the words simmered.

I ran to the shadows
to grab buckets of water,
cowered in wet clothes
to ward off their rage.

How can this fear be stilled
forgotten, when today
my door jams open, listening?
Dark memories ignite the sparks.

I hold ash now
as a way to remember,
to not cling on
to open wounds.

UNRAVELLING

You're sat glazed and I'm wondering
who shaped this air?
They've taken each part, each stitch
from your body and sewn in blank words.
Can you hear me now?
I need to unravel these clothes,
cut, tear, break these new seams
and heave your old self back
to this chair.
Rest with me, where you used to sew
threading yourself into skirts, dresses and minds.
We can unpick together,
these clothes weren't made for you.
I'll help you find your words.
The green catches my eye
and soft yellows show life
does not age outside.
Can you hear me now?
Somewhere inside lies your spark
and I'm trying to reach it,
cut, tear, wrench these outer layers
and find you there,
pleading to be let out.

IS THIS THE FUTURE?

There are empty chapters on your face,
the haul of today found nothing —
every hour lost.

It's like someone stole the photos,
took the words from the dictionary
and ran away with your voice.

You wonder where you are.
You wonder who we are.
I wonder who I am.

Who have I become
when I can't finish that phrase,
when a hot flush has me grounded?

I carry menopause,
watch the roughness of my skin crack
when I hold on to being young.

I know the sharp claws of a voice,
the dull hours at night,
the heavy pound of fatigue.

When I watch your failing body
I compare it to mine —
is that where I'm heading?

HOLD FIRE

I wonder if you're there at your window
watching the world find its eyes,
where the lambs used to roam free
on the best natural playground?

The nettle paths you steered me clear of
the berry feasts I couldn't eat.
We used to walk to grow ideas,
until the builders shovelled our peace.

Are you there now, reading this?
It's different you tell me:
clattering noise has shattered glass —
a slice in moist eyes.

I must stop. I don't mean to upset
but I thought of you last night —
a blazing sunset fixed sparks in my eyes.
Did you see?

We'd always marvel holding our breath.
They can't take the sky.
Look out of your window and I will mine —
together, we can hold fire.

FINDING OUR CURE

I would tear down your wall
and bring you back,
if I could buy the right tools.

I would reach inside your mind,
rip out the blockage
and help you walk free.

I would fly with you
back to when we were young,
before we knew we'd get so ill.

You could teach me how to sew,
how you made all those clothes –
I'd get it right this time.

We could race down the track
find out who really was the fastest,
be free from these useless legs we now drag.

Those days you can't remember
show them to me, take me there,
then we'll know.

If we could spend one more day
in our young and healthy bodies,
we'd get it right this time.

ACKNOWLEDGEMENTS

Thank you to the editors of the following publications in which some of these poems have appeared:

Control, Ink Sweat & Tears, *Swamp*, The Honest Ulsterman, *Unravelling*, Skylight47, *Wolf Class*, Acropolis Journal, *Relief*, *Sun Snake*, *My Next Move*, The Hedgehog Poetry Press, *Earthquake*, Dreich, *Autograph Book*, Fevers of the Mind, *Them*, Flights e-Journal, *Hold Fire*, Black Nore Review and *Full of Green*, Fragmented Voices.

Sun Snake was a winning poem in *The Hedgehog Poetry Press* Summer Challenge, 2022.

Huge thanks to my family, friends and medical personnel who have been a constant support.

To Steve Logan who has helped me find a way through the challenges I encounter and who's knowledge of poetry is beyond words.

To Carole Bromley, Steve Logan and Lucy Heuschen for spending their precious time with this book and writing such thoughtful comments.

Thank you to Steve Logan, Anna Saunders, CB1 Poetry, Cambridge Stanza, The Bridge Poets, St Ives, The Commemoration Hall poetry group, Huntingdon and all my friends on Zoom who have given incredible mentoring, guidance and feedback on these poems. To Niche Comics Bookshop, Huntingdon for your wonderful support.

I'd like to give particular thanks to Mark Davidson, editor of The Hedgehog Poetry Press for believing in these poems.

Find out more about Julie's work at www.jumpingjulespoetry.com

Julie will make a donation to the MS Trust charity based on the proceeds from the sale of this collection.